Long Live
the King

Johnny Hart and
Brant Parker

CORONET BOOKS
Hodder Fawcett, London

Copyright © 1970 Field Newspaper Syndicate
Copyright © 1975 Fawcett Publications Inc.

First published in the United States 1975
by Fawcett Publications Inc.

Coronet edition 1975
Fifth impression 1981

Printed in Great Britain for Hodder
Fawcett Ltd., Mill Road, Dunton Green,
Sevenoaks, Kent (Editorial Office:
47 Bedford Square, London, WC1 3DP) by
Hunt Barnard Printing Ltd.,
Aylesbury, Bucks.

ISBN 0 340 20529 6

1-26

Z-10

2

BANG BANG HIT HAMMER SCRAPE SCRAPE

IT'S FINISHED! THE GREATEST INVENTION SINCE THE WHEEL!

2-25

WHAT IS IT?

THE AXLE.

THE KING IS RUNNING A LOOK-ALIKE CONTEST.

WHAT DOES THE WINNER GET?

3-4

HE GETS TO RIDE UP FRONT WITH THE DRIVER WHEN THE COACH PASSES THROUGH THE GHETTO.

SIRE, THERE IS A REPRESENTATIVE OF THE NEWS MEDIA HERE TO SEE YOU.

OH, *GOOD*... SHOW HIM IN!

3-9

WHEN ARE YOU GOING TO PAY YOUR BILL?

NEWS

3-20

3-25

CAREFUL...
HE COULD BE
PLAYING
POSSUM!

4-1

I'M HUNGRY ENOUGH TO EAT A HORSE!

GOOD.

4-4

4-8

AMAZING!...
JUGGLING SIX
WINE BOTTLES
WITHOUT A GOOF...
HOW DOES HE
DO IT?

...THEY'RE
FULL.

4-10

How to make rain.
(turn to page 46)

FLIP
FLIP
FLIP
FLIP
FLIP

4-13

5

I'VE ISOLATED THE COLD VIRUS!

HOW DO YOU KNOW IT'S THE COLD VIRUS?

BECAUSE ITS NOSE IS RUNNING.

4-25

5-1

54

5-11

6

5-13

5-19

BARTENDER! A DRINK FOR MY FRIENDS!

5-20

WOULD YOU CARE TO MAKE THAT ACQUAINTANCES?

5-21

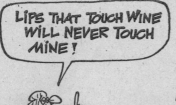

6-6

7

HOW ARE YOU DOING IN THE STOCK MARKET?

I JUST BOUGHT 100 SHARES OF AMALGAMATED MINES.

6-16

MY BROKER TOLD ME THEY SHOULD SPLIT SOON.

SOONER THAN YOU **THINK** ... I SAW THEM BOARDING UP THE MINE, THIS MORNING.

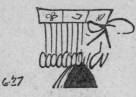

6-27

6-29

7-6

EVERYONE'S GOT THE RICKETS, EXCEPT THE STOREKEEPER.

WHO'S THAT?

BUNG.

WHAT'S **HIS** SECRET?

DAIQUIRIS.

7-11

7-15

7-16

THOSE BLASTED PEASANTS ARE LATE FOR WORK AGAIN!

7-29

BUT, SIRE...THEY HAVE BEEN WORKING TWENTY HOURS A DAY!

SO...

...THAT LEAVES THEM FOUR HOURS TO GET TO WORK.

B.C. IT'S A FUNNY WORLD

JOHNNY HART

☐ 21248 9	B.C. Dip In The Road	75p
☐ 19474 X	B.C. Right On	75p
☐ 16881 1	What's New B.C.	75p
☐ 18780 8	B.C. Is Alive and Well	75p
☐ 25066 6	B.C. Where The Hell Is Heck	65p
☐ 20762 0	B.C. It's A Funny World	60p
☐ 16477 8	Back To B.C.	75p

JOHNNY HART AND BRANT PARKER

☐ 16476 X	The Peasants Are Revolting	60p
☐ 16899 4	Remember The Golden Rule	75p
☐ 25679 6	Wizard Of Id Charge	65p
☐ 18604 6	There's A Fly In My Swill	75p

All these books are available at your local bookshop or newsagent, or can be ordered direct from the publisher. Just tick the titles you want and fill in the form below.

Prices and availability subject to change without notice.

CORONET BOOKS, P.O. Box 11, Falmouth, Cornwall.

Please send cheque or postal order, and allow the following for postage and packing:

U.K. – 40p for one book, plus 18p for the second book, and 13p for each additional book ordered up to a £1.49 maximum.

B.F.P.O. and EIRE – 40p for the first book, plus 18p for the second book, and 13p per copy for the next 7 books, 7p per book thereafter.

OTHER OVERSEAS CUSTOMERS – 60p for the first book, plus 18p per copy for each additional book.

Name ....

Address ....

....